THE BASICS OF
BUSINESS
WRITING

MARTY STUCKEY

amacom
AMERICAN MANAGEMENT ASSOCIATION
THE WORKSMART SERIES

Library of Congress Cataloging-in-Publication Data

Stuckey, Marty.
    The basics of business writing / Marty Stuckey.
      p.   cm.—(The WorkSmart series)

    ISBN 0-8144-7792-5
    1. Business writing. I. Title. II. Series.
  HF5718.3.S78   1992
808'.06665–dc20   91–42689
                                   CIP

Printing number

10

CONTENTS

PREFACE

Nothing so terrorizes so many otherwise competent adults as the prospect of having to write something (unless it's having to make a speech, which when you think about it, isn't really very different). They think of thirty-eight things they have to do first. They clean their desk, catch up on their phone calls, sharpen their pencil (figuratively or literally), pull out all their background files and a few others just in case . . . everything possible to postpone the moment of truth: facing the blank page (or computer screen).

FEAR OF WRITING

Fear of writing originates from some serious misconceptions:

- That writing is hard or mysterious, or both
- That writing is a form of English significantly different from common speech
- That writing skill is a gift that some people have and some don't

Words fly, writings remain. (Litera scripta manet, verbum ut inane perit.)

—LATIN PROVERB

The tragedy is that this fear becomes self-fulfilling: Too many people end up writing badly because they are afraid to write simply.

I'm going to let you in on a secret: Good writing is simple. Not that it is necessarily simple to create (although it is simpler than you think), but that the end product is simple, not complex. There is nothing more powerful than a straightforward sentence made up of ordinary words. If you doubt this, compare any paragraph at random from the last memo you received with any paragraph written by Hemingway or the apostle Paul, and ask yourself which is easier to understand and remember.

Trying to write "right" is what paralyzes many people. The solution is to lighten up. This book will show you ways to loosen up your writing, and so take the fear out of the process.

What This Book Is Not

- *This is not a recipe book, with sample formats for different types of documents.* We will not spend much time on the specifics of different end products: reports, memos, letters, documentation, spec sheets, proposals, minutes of meetings, employee manuals, and so on.

We will study many examples of documents from different industries (real documents with the names of companies and individuals changed). But primarily we will focus on process and technique. To a very great extent, the principles of good writing apply universally; once you master them, you can use them in all your writing projects.

- *This is not a style guide.* There are a number of good references that catechize questions of style, usage, and presentation: *The Chicago Manual of Style*, the *AP Style Guide*, *Words Into Type*, and the *Government Printing Office Style Guide* are among the best known. It is possible the word processing managers in your organization have already selected one as your company bible. In any case, this particular wheel already exists.

- *This is not a textbook on grammar, spelling, or syntax.* Rules of punctuation or grammar *in and of themselves* are not worth a used typewriter ribbon. In this book, we will concern ourselves with what is important:

  - Organizing your ideas
  - Getting started with the task of writing
  - Producing a document that is both logical and lively
  - Eliminating roadblocks to understanding

To be sure, that last item is wide-ranging. Potential roadblocks are everywhere, although some of them are quite small:

  - If punctuation is so unconventional that readers stumble, that's important.

- If grammatical errors make you look like a dope, that's important.
- If you use the wrong word and produce an entirely different meaning from what you intended, that's important.

If those things get in the way of your reader getting your message, and *getting it on the first pass,* then you have a problem and you need to learn the "right" way.

But we are not going to deal with these things as niceties for their own sake. We will not engage in esoteric wrangling over the fine shades of meaning in a particular word. We will not debate subtle questions of syntax that have two right answers. We will not struggle over the complexities of punctuation. There is nothing sillier than mature adults arguing over semicolons.

What You Will Learn

- The critical connection between writing and time

- The four benchmarks that define good business writing:

1. It achieves its purpose.
2. It is clear.
3. It engages the reader's attention.
4. It is enjoyable to read.

- A four-step process that alleviates the agony of writing:

1. Plan.
2. Write.
3. Polish.
4. Format.

- How to grade yourself on your next writing project

- Fingertip guides: antiquated phrases to avoid, common spelling errors, words that are often confused, resources for further information

GOOD WRITING IS CLEAR WRITING

In the business world, "good" equals "clear." Good, clear writing has two main components: the words on the paper (the part you see) and the thinking behind them (the part you do not see). And *both* need to be right. Mistakes in one area can wipe out the effectiveness in all other areas.

You can do a masterful job of organizing your ideas and presenting your conclusions, but if you do it with lots of misspelled words, you might as well not have bothered, for you have ruined your credibility. On the other hand, you can produce a report that gets an A-plus on mechanics from your ninth-grade English teacher, but if the logic is muddled, no one will make the effort to wade through it.

Learn to write well, or not to write at all.

—JOHN DRYDEN

Beautiful creative writing (fiction, nonfiction, poetry) is an art. It sparkles, it glows, it moves us to tears, it sneaks up on us with a devastating punch. *Word* + *word* + *word* = magic.

Good, clear business writing is a craft. It informs, it summarizes, it persuades. *Word* + *word* + *word* = good information. This kind of writing comes easier to some people than to others, but anyone willing to make the effort will find that it can be learned, improved, and mastered. And in mastery, business writing can approach art.

M.S.

CHAPTER 1

THE REAL PROBLEM
WITH BUSINESS WRITING

How many times has this happened to you: You start to read a document (letter, memo, report), pause, frown, say to yourself, "Huh?" and go back to the beginning and start reading again? Several thousand times? A few million?

What's the problem here? Maybe you think, "This person doesn't know how to say what he means." Or you may blame yourself: "I just can't understand what this is all about." But the real problem is not the other person's ability to write or your ability to understand. *The core issue is the time wasted when you had to read it twice.*

Good writing is not about formats, commas, or even specific words. At rock bottom, the whole issue of writing well—at least in the business world—is about *time:*

Writing time + reading time = total communication time

1. The time it takes you to write something
2. The time it takes others to read and understand it

The two are directly related: The less time you put into your writing, the more time others will have to put into understanding it.

TIME INVESTMENT THAT PAYS OFF

Whose time do you want to save? Yours or the reader's? If you answered, "Mine," think again.

Suppose you're writing to your boss—do you really want to waste her time?

Or to a customer—do you really want to antagonize him with something he can't understand?

Or to your staff—do you really want them to collectively scratch their heads trying to figure out what you want done?

Or to colleagues—do you really want them to say, "Oh no, another memo from Jim"?

If you're going to answer the question from a self-centered perspective, consider this: Top executives consistently name "good writing skills" as a key talent they look for in their people. If for no other reason than your own advancement, you need to learn how to write effectively.

Why should you bother learning how to write well? Because writing poorly costs you dearly.

Yes, it takes time to write a clear, logical, persuasive document. But writing a bad document takes much more time in the long run.

A FABLE ABOUT WRITING

Let me tell you a story about one memo and four people. Assume that all four people are average writers whose salary ranges are appropriate for your industry. As the story unfolds, try to estimate the cost in time and dollars at each step.

1. Chris, a mid-level manager, writes a two-page memo to Dale, another manager.

2. Because of the nature of this memo, Chris decides it needs to be typed on company letterhead and copied to three other people: Clarence, Raphael, and Alice. His assistant types and circulates the memo.

3. Dale receives Chris's memo in the morning mail along with quite a few others. She reads it once, doesn't understand it, and sets it aside.

4. The next day, Dale picks up the memo and has to read it all again. She concludes that some information is missing, so she writes her own memo to Chris, asking for

clarification. She sends copies of her memo to the other three original addresses.

5. Chris receives the memo from Dale, reads it quickly, and fires back an answer.

6. Dale reads the second memo, realizes Chris misunderstood her question, and tries to telephone him for clarification. He's not in, so she opts to write a second query.

7. In the meantime, Raphael thinks he knows the answer to Dale's question, so he sends off a quick note to her.

8. Raphael also has his own question for Chris, so he writes a memo about it and cc's the other three recipients.

9. To save time, Chris answers Raphael's question by sending a duplicate copy of his answer to Dale's question (see step #5).

10. Raphael reads that answer too quickly, not noticing that it's addressed to Dale, and finds it very confusing. He concludes that Chris is a total idiot and resolves to try to avoid him. What is the cost of the maneuvers Raphael will have to make to avoid working with Chris?

11. When Clarence gets Chris's original memo, he scans it, concludes it doesn't really relate to him, and tosses it aside. Unfortunately, it concerns a decision he needs to participate in. What is the cost of Clarence's absence?

12. Meanwhile, Alice puzzles over Chris's original memo. On second reading, she decides it is a request for some background information. Since Chris is above her in the hierarchy, she immediately gets to work producing something that Chris does not need.

When ideas fail, words come in handy.

—Johann Wolfgang von Goethe

In the manner of all fables, this one is exaggerated slightly, for emphasis. But anyone who has ever worked in an organization will recognize its painful truths.

Think of all the time and money wasted. What do you think of Chris's chances for promotion?

A TRUE STORY ABOUT WRITING

1. On February 24, a project manager in Los Angeles wrote a memo to an operations manager in San Francisco,

describing a proposed change in an internal procedure that would involve software redesign. That memo was carbon-copied (cc'ed) to five others.

2. On March 19, the San Francisco manager responded with a two-page memo that began "We have reviewed the 'Proposal to Modify CWS' and have questions as to the details of the proposed changes." She then enumerated ten very specific questions. The "cc" list at the bottom had the names of three people plus an item called "branch participants"; the attached list of branch participants comprised seventeen names. So in addition to the person it was primarily addressed to, twenty people got the second memo.

3. On March 22, the Los Angeles manager, with the assistance of the quality assurance manager, prepared a response to the ten questions (adding some other thoughts, too). That memo was four single-spaced pages and was addressed to the San Francisco manager with carbon copies to five others.

4. On March 25, all the San Francisco people got together to talk about the proposal.

5. On April 1, all twenty-two people involved up to this point participated in a conference call. The original proposer was asked for still more information.

6. On April 5, the Los Angeles manager prepared the requested material (which constituted four pages) and assembled a package with copies of all the documents that had preceded it, along with a cover memo. The new package—fourteen pages—was sent to the San Francisco manager and cc'ed to five others.

I don't know how many other memos were written before the final decision was made, but I do know that the proposed change never took place.

YOUR OWN WRITING INVESTMENT

Think of the last memo or interoffice letter you wrote. Suppose you dashed through it too hurriedly, like Chris, and sent it to three people.

Writing time:	1 hour
Reading time:	6 hours (3 people, 2 hours each to read, struggle through, set aside, read again)
Total communications time:	7 hours

By contrast, what might have happened if you had doubled your writing time?

Writing time:	2 hours
Reading time:	1.5 hours (.5 hour each for 3 people)
Total communication time:	3.5 hours
Savings in raw time:	3.5 hours (nothing to sneeze at)
Savings in reputation:	immeasurable

And now for the good news: Once you learn the process of writing that is described in this book, you can write a clear document in the same time it used to take you to write a fuzzy one—and probably a good deal less. So you end up saving your time and everyone else's. Nice work.

CHAPTER 2

THE BIG PICTURE

Good business writing is writing that works—it does what it is supposed to do. Every rule that anyone tells you about writing is subordinate to this one: Writing is communication. The best writing is that which most effectively communicates the necessary message and no more.

But exactly what makes business writing effective?

WHAT MAKES GOOD WRITING GOOD?

Good writing:

- ☑ Achieves its purpose.
- ☑ Is clear.
- ☑ Engages attention.
- ☑ Is enjoyable to read.

The difficulty of the writing process is that these elements are interconnected in many subtle and not so subtle ways.

Achieving a Purpose

All writing has a purpose. When that purpose is fulfilled, the writing has done its job. This is not as simple as it sounds. The real purpose may be hidden beneath a tangle of personal idiosyncrasies, office politics, and the prior history of the situation. Focusing on one key objective requires a considerable amount of thought.

Being Clear

A good piece of writing has to be clear on several levels:

Level 1: The Entire Document. The overall nature of the communication must be clearly evident. This means that the people receiving it should be able to tell immediately what it is about.

Level 2: Each Subsection. The important ideas, the main "chunks" that constitute the overall message, have to be presented in a sequence so clear and logical that they lead inevitably to only one conclusion.

Level 3: Each Paragraph. Each paragraph should clearly follow from the preceding material. The reader should be able to track the course and not have to look back.

Level 4: Each Sentence. Each individual sentence should express its thought so directly that it cannot be misunderstood, even by someone reading hastily.

As a practical matter, clarity is the result of (1) good organization (see Chapter 3) and (2) straightforward writing style (see Chapter 5).

Engaging Attention

Sometimes the urgency of a situation may compel people to read a document even if it is boring . . . but don't count on it. Most of the time, you have to consciously find ways to keep the reader's attention.

Being Enjoyable to Read

Everything that can be said can be said clearly.

—LUDWIG WITTGENSTEIN

Good writing is pleasant to read (or, at least, not unpleasant). With good writing, readers are not bogged down in long-winded explanations. Their eyes don't glaze over from tracking torturous sentences. They are not clichéd to death. And they do not get rear-ended by startling errors in spelling, punctuation, or grammar.

So the task in this area is twofold: (1) Write strong sentences with strong words. (2) Avoid errors that set your reader's teeth

SAD BUT TRUE

The person reading what you wrote cares less about it than you do.

on edge. Except for errors of mechanics, this is really about style: "Write with your ears." But in spite of what you might think, there are specific guidelines that are relatively easy to master. You may not become Barbara Tuchman or Wallace Stegner, but then there are no Pulitzer Prizes for business writing. Yet.

DO YOU REALLY NEED TO WRITE THIS?

One of the first things to decide is, do you need to write this document at all? This is not always easy. We are all shaped by habit, and too many of us are infected with "memoitis" or "reportitis" or whatever "itis" virus is most common in your industry. In many offices people's worth is measured by the number and length of memos they write. And now that electronic mail is a common feature in most offices, we find it all too easy to write a message when some other medium would be better.

When Not to Write

Sometimes it's better not to write. Here are some very general guidelines. They may or may not be appropriate in your own situation, but perhaps they will start you thinking.

1. When you need a piece of information from someone who has it in his or her head (that is, doesn't need to look anything up), make a simple phone call.

2. When the situation is delicate and you need to feel your way along, it's better to have a conversation face-to-face so you can watch the other person's reactions.

3. When several people are involved in a decision, get them all together and hash it out rather than start an endless round of memos.

4. When you have already covered the situation in person or on the phone; for example, any letter or memo that begins "Confirming our conversation of April 12, . . ." is quite likely unnecessary.

5. When your intuition tells you that you don't want

something recorded on paper, a memo is unwise. Written words follow us around—just ask any presidential appointee who has endured the process of Senate confirmation hearings.

But let's assume you have evaluated the situation and decided that some form of written communication is appropriate. Now what should you do?

A PROCESS THAT WORKS

Here's what not to do: Sit down, write until you've said everything you can think of, and then send off the finished product.

Practically no one can create a cogent, persuasive document on the first pass. And practically everyone tries to. The end result: a document that is too long, too jumbled, too wordy, unorganized, unfocused, and, ultimately, unread.

The human brain processes information and thoughts in complex and dazzling ways. One part of your brain enables you to put thoughts into words. Another part enables you to sequence ideas into a logical order. Two different brain functions are involved. The practicality is, therefore, that you cannot write and plan at the same time. Still another part of your brain enables you to critique and evaluate. This means that you cannot write and edit yourself at the same time. This book is built around a writing process that recognizes these different brain functions and aims to work with them, not against them.

The process has four discrete parts:

1. Plan your writing.
2. Write the first draft.
3. Edit and correct your draft.
4. Design the visual format for ease of reading.

Good writers know that planning takes more time than any of the other steps in the writing process.

If you're doing everything right, step 1 should take considerably more time than steps 2 and 4, and somewhat more time than step 3. The actual amount of time, in accumulated minutes, will of course vary with the type of project. Planning a full proposal, after all, takes longer than planning a one-page letter. But the process should always involve the same sequence of steps.

In the next four chapters, we'll walk through each of these four steps in some detail.

CHAPTER 3

STEP 1:
PLANNING YOUR WRITING

If any man
wishes to
write a
clear style,
let him
first be
clear in his
thoughts.

—JOHANN
WOLFGANG
VON GOETHE

If your writing is to achieve its purpose, you must know whom you're writing to, and why. You must know what you want to accomplish, and you must achieve it using language and tone that are appropriate to the purpose and the audience. You must include everything your reader needs to know and no more. In other words: Plan first, write second.

Does the idea of sitting down to plan before putting words on the paper strike you as wasted energy? If so, it's time for a reminder: The time you put into planning saves times in the long run—by a factor of at least two.

Think of it this way: Someone is going to have to go through the process of assembling ideas and information, sifting through and weeding out, and ordering them into a sequence that leads naturally to a certain conclusion. Either you do it at the front end, or your reader will have to do it at the back end. If the reader does it, and most won't even bother, you have lost control over the conclusions they will reach.

There is one other benefit: *You* save time. When you take the time to plan, the total time needed to produce the document is reduced.

Exactly what does the planning process involve? Well, you may spend more time staring at the walls than writing. Mostly, it involves asking yourself some very pointed questions:

- Why am I writing?
- Whom am I writing to?
- What kind of piece should I write?

- What action step do I want as a result?
- What tone is right for the piece?
- What are all the points I could conceivably make about this subject?
- Out of those, what points *should* I make, and in what order?

Ordered into a linear sequence, the elements of the planning step are:

1. Clarify the purpose.
2. Analyze the audience.
3. Decide on a strategy (type of document, action step, tone).
4. Determine the content.

CLARIFY THE PURPOSE: WHY AM I WRITING?

Failure to make the purpose clear is one of the most common problems with business writing. The recipient doesn't know what to do because there's no obvious "peg" to grab onto. And that peg is missing because the writer of the document didn't take the time to think the purpose through, or to spell it out, or both.

Your purpose in writing the document translates into what you want your readers to do, so don't keep it a secret.

Problem: Purpose Is Missing

Dear Marian,

Following our conversation this week, I found that this revision of the deposit plan is not one that is under the gun for government reasons, and therefore I think that it is going to be necessary to have a review of these proposed remarks and to bring it up to date.

If you received this memo, could you tell what it's about and what you're being asked to do? Ignore the twisted syntax for now; just ask yourself if you can deduce the main purpose.

To get what you want, you have to know what you want. The burden is always with the writer. Ask yourself, "What do I want to have happen as a result of someone reading this?" The answer to that question is your purpose.

> "I want the authority to hire two temporary people."
> "I want to know if our application forms have to be changed."
> "I want department heads to return the payroll forms on time."
> "I want our employees to retain a positive outlook even though we're making some cutbacks."
> "I want this person's job performance in this particular area to improve."

Sometimes you have to peel back another layer or two to get to the truth.

> "I want to present the results of my research."
> No you don't. You want something specific to happen.
> "Okay, I want my boss to be aware of what the research indicates."
> But why? For what purpose?
> "I think the research points to one best alternative, and I want the boss to reach that conclusion too so he will sign off and tell us to go ahead in that direction."

There you go!

In addition to the surface situation, there may be a hidden purpose or two. For instance: You want to announce a department reorganization, but you also want the employees to transfer their loyalty to the new boss. The more complicated the situation is, the more questions you have to ask yourself.

Clear Purpose, Clearly Stated

John Stringer informs me that he has a pile of data on the drift problem. Please attend a hopefully brief meeting to discuss what, if anything, we are going to do with these data.

SAD BUT TRUE

Your reader can read your document but not your mind.

When: Thursday, May 9, at 9 A.M.
Where: John Stringer's old desk, in the Bridge
area.
Thanks.

Here's an example of what happens when the writer does not take the time to figure out the purpose.

Problem: The Purpose Is Unclear

[The six-page, single-spaced report headed "Daily Accounting" opens with this paragraph:]

> There appear to be a number of ways to look at daily accounting. I will attempt to define what we mean by daily accounting, as well as providing the attached articles which further discuss daily accounting.

So, the stated purpose is to (a) define a term and (b) pass along some supporting articles. Four pages later, we find this paragraph:

> It seems to me that our challenge is to be in a position to provide the same capabilities should our clients be willing to purchase them. It seems abundantly clear that this is the direction in which the industry is migrating. Our sales folks report that daily accounting is beginning to be a critical item in proposal presentation and ultimate provider selection.

Aha! A clue. The core message seems to be: "Our competitors are doing this; we should be too." Maybe the purpose is: "I want to update you on an important trend in our market." Next paragraph:

> I am aware of three vendors of turnkey daily accounting software. I would suggest that we begin to gather information from these vendors on their specific systems as we begin to deal with the strategic issue of how we should approach daily accounting.

Another clue. In other words, what is our strategy about daily accounting going to be? Maybe the purpose is: "I want the company to define its strategy on this issue." Secondary purpose: "I want you to appoint someone to research the three vendors." The final paragraph:

> It seems clear to me that we will not move exclusively to a daily accounting system. I believe we will continue to provide the type of services we currently provide while supplementing with daily accounting when appropriate.

But wait: After raising the question of strategy, the writer seems to be answering it. "We'll add this service but keep the ones we now have." So was this the purpose: "I want to explain the strategy I have determined"? Who knows?

The problem is not that this report is too long but that it is unfocused. The writer seems to have dumped everything he knows about daily accounting into one memo, just in case. He seems to have no clear idea of his purpose or intended audience. Remember, the stated purpose of the memo was to define a term and provide some reading material. If the people receiving the memo already knew the definition, would they be inclined to keep reading? Six pages' worth?

ANALYZE THE AUDIENCE: TO WHOM AM I WRITING?

Along with defining a clear purpose, you must define your audience. The two go hand in hand. Why? Because together they will determine what you say, how much, and how.

Ask yourself, "Whom am I writing this for? And what do I know about them?" This question is usually much easier to answer than the question about purpose. The problem is, too few people take the time to ask it.

You need to be aware of the following facts:

☑ Whom should I be addressing this to?
☑ Who else might read it?

☑ How much about the situation do they already know?

☑ How much technical background in the field do they have?

☑ Do they already have an opinion about this situation?

☑ What do I know about their prejudices?

SAD BUT TRUE

You are writing for your boss, your colleagues, your customers, not yourself. Write what they need to know, not what you want to say.

If the document you are creating is long, or crucial, it's a good idea to write down the answers to those questions.

You may have more than one audience—this is common. You may have one reader initially and other potential readers in the future. Nevertheless, you most likely have one primary reader. Just make sure you know who that is.

The one person you are not writing for is yourself.

DECIDE ON A STRATEGY

What Kind of Document Should I Write?

Quite often, this is self-evident. If you're writing to someone outside the company, you need a letter. If you're writing in response to an agency's RFP (request for a proposal), you will prepare a proposal.

But when you are communicating with others within the organization, you may need to stop and think:

- Should I send a formal memo or a casual E-mail message?
- Should I write a brief review or a full report?
- Should I write a short memo describing my request or develop the full proposal?

What Action Step Should I Ask For?

You're much more likely to get what you want if you ask for it, plainly and directly. Too many business writers stop short of this step: They do not state the explicit action step they are seeking.

But if you take the time during the planning stage to raise this question, you'll ensure that you include this important element in your finished document.

The technique involves asking yourself another question. *"Exactly what do I want this person to do next, and when and how?"*

The action step is narrower than the purpose. The purpose is the overall end result you hope for. The action step is what you want to see happen next. Examples of weak and strong action steps follow.

> *Weak action step:* "Please review this proposal and contact me with your response at your earliest convenience."
> *Strong action step:* "I would really like to have your ideas on this. Could we have lunch next week? I'll call you Tuesday morning to see how your schedule looks."

> *Weak action step:* "Please forward this information as soon as possible."
> *Strong action step:* "Our report is due to Mr. Thompson on May 15, so ideally I'd like to have your department numbers by the 13th. Is this possible?"
> *Stronger action step:* "Our time frame is tight, and our project manager tells me we will need all the departmental numbers by May 13. I'll call you next Monday to make sure we are on track."

Problem: Action Step Is Not Specific

I particularly am wanting to know the answer that will undoubtedly be coming as to whether or not anything can be done to a person's plan through the courts. Your help would be appreciated.

What Kind of Tone Should I Use?

When we're talking with someone face-to-face, we communicate our meaning through our tone of voice, inflection, and facial expressions, as well as with the actual words we say. The person we are talking to would have no difficulty distinguishing between these two statements:

> "That's a great idea." (snide and sarcastic)
> "That's a great idea!" (congratulatory, sincere)

This is because the tone is so different.

In written communication, you don't have gesture, expression, or inflection to help convey your meaning. You must rely on words alone. That is why the *tone* of the piece you write is so important.

Tone is the document's overall emotional temperature: warm, friendly, chatty, businesslike, firm, cool, distant, accusatory, funny, simplistic, scholarly, angry, and so forth. It is not what you say, but how you say it. It is the end product of the specific words you choose, and the way you put them together.

Problem: Tone Is Offensive

> Attached is a listing of accounting jobs submitted by your area which have failed in the last week. Each of these failures incurs the following overhead:
>
> [Writer goes on to list four separate paragraph items, and concludes:]
>
> The following chart shows common failures which repeatedly occur in your unit. All these could be eliminated by ensuring operating department users understand and follow proper job submission procedures.
>
> Please call me with questions or call Angela Basent to request training from the Accounting Department.

The core message is "errors are expensive, and we need to work together to try to reduce them." But the particular words the writer used also convey, because of their negative, accusatory tone, an underlying message: "Your operators make too many mistakes and it causes us a lot of extra work. Can't you control your people? Maybe you need some training." Did he really intend to say, "You're all a bunch of dopes over there"? Probably not, but that's the tone of his memo.

Be especially conscious of tone when sending electronic mail. One advantage of E-mail is that it is instantaneous. That is also its disadvantage. It is so easy to use that too many people shoot from the hip: They read a message and respond immediately, without pausing to think how to word their reply. From the sender's point of view, it's like talking. But from the receiver's perspective, it's like reading: They will pick up the hidden message that your tone conveys just as surely as if you had typed it on engraved stationery.

The great art in writing well is to know when to stop.

—Josh Billings

DETERMINE THE CONTENT: WHAT SHOULD I INCLUDE?

The next big step in planning is deciding what to say. That in itself is a three-step process:

1. Gather all the ideas, facts, or theories that pertain to the message.
2. Sort through the lot, weeding out unnecessary items.

PROJECT WORKSHEET

Think about a specific writing project you have coming up soon. Let's walk through the steps we have covered so far in the planning process.

My purpose is _____

I am addressing this piece to _____
who is [important points about this person that affect your planning] _____

I am going to write a [type of document] _____
because _____

The action step I will ask for is _____

Considering whom I'm writing to and why, I think the best tone is _____

3. Organize what is left into a logical sequence that works.

It's a bit like fishing with a gill net: You put the net out and see what gets caught in it. Later you go through everything and decide what to keep and what to throw back in the water.

Gathering Ideas: Brainstorming by Yourself

No doubt you are familiar with the idea-generating technique known as brainstorming: Several people get together and talk something through in a verbal free-for-all, each idea triggering several others. When you are wrestling with the very complex question of what to include in your document, you can use the same basic technique. Only in this case you are brainstorming with yourself. There are several mechanical ways to do this.

Brainstorming on Paper

Step 1. Take a blank sheet of paper and turn it sideways.

Step 2. Draw a circle in the middle, and write—in one or two words—the basic purpose of the document you are planning (see Figure 1).

Step 3. All around that circle, write the names of associated ideas, in as few words as possible. Don't worry about where they are located in relation to the main circle or to each other; just write them down quickly, as you think of them. Keep going until you can't think of anything more (see Figure 2).

Step 4. Using colored markers, draw smaller circles

Figure 1. Brainstorming: step 1.

Figure 2. Brainstorming: step 2.

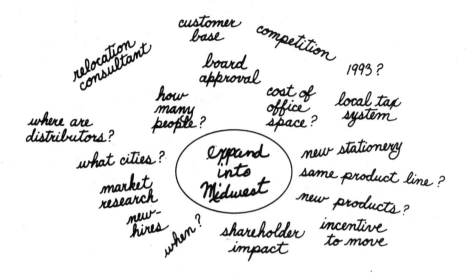

around all those points. Assign one color to each main category. For example, everything that has to do with manufacturing processes is circled in green; all the benefits are circled in blue.

Variations on a Theme

1. "Mind mapping": After writing the main idea in a circle, extend "branches" from it for main subtopics, and mini branches from the main branches for points that relate to each subtopic.

2. Using 3 × 5 cards: Write down all the points you can think of and then arrange the cards into clusters.

3. Using small Post-It notes: Write down all the points you can think of and arrange the notes on a large piece of paper or on the wall where you're writing (see Figure 3).

Sorting Through the Ideas

Now you must decide: Which of those points do I really need to include in my document? Remind yourself of two very important items you have already worked on: (1) What is my purpose? (2) Who is my reader?

Point by point, look at your brainstorm sheet, mind map, or stack of cards. For each one, ask yourself:

Figure 3.   A mind map.

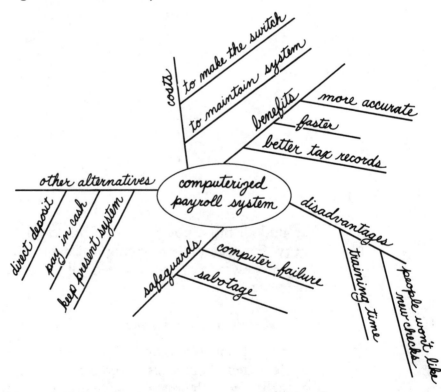

Words differently arranged have a different meaning, and meanings differently arranged have different effects.

—PASCAL

- Does this further my purpose?
- Does my reader need me to spell it out?

Whenever you get a "no," cross that item out. Be ruthless. Don't recap the entire analysis process you went through unless it clearly contributes to your purpose and your reader is unaware of it. Don't include things just to show off how much you know; you're not writing for yourself, but for your reader.

Organizing Ideas

Now take the remaining ideas and organize them into a sequence. This means that both logic and strategy must be considered.

- Logic: Point A leads to point B which leads to point C which leads to the conclusion.
- Strategy: Where would point A have the most impact? Does the conclusion go at the end or the beginning?

Be sure your plan assigns a place for (1) Your purpose in writing (put it near the beginning, perhaps the first sentence) and (2) The action step you desire (either the beginning or end).

At this point—and not before—you may want to rewrite the points into an outline structure:

I. Main point
   A. Secondary item
      1. Supporting item

The Last Word

When people have trouble deciding what to include in their writing, they usually wrestle with the temptation to put in too much. However, it is not uncommon for people to put in too little, especially if they are writing quickly. Sometimes we know so clearly what we mean, we think we already said it.

Problem: Key Point Left Out

[The entire message is reproduced here.]

In their efforts to streamline the Annual Reports and application processes, the good folks at the IRS require us to use computer scannable forms. The entries on these forms must fit into prescribed spaces. Entries extending beyond the prescribed spaces can cause the form to be rejected/returned/etc.

Therefore, please try to curb the imaginative excesses of some of our clients, prospective and otherwise, regarding the names of their retirement plan. Everyone will be better served by brevity. Thanks.

But just how long can the names be? The writer forgot to tell us.

CHAPTER 4

STEP 2:
WRITING THE FIRST DRAFT

Words are what hold society together.

—STUART CHASE

The moment of truth is here. Time to start writing. Now what?

Scene 1: Panicked Person Starts to Write

Panicked Paul holds pen in tight grip and frowns at blank paper. After agonizing minutes, he begins to write his first sentence. He stops in the middle, "No, that doesn't sound good." He crosses out words and starts over. In the second sentence, he pauses: "What was that guy's name from the Pasadena office?" He goes to look up the name. In third sentence, another pause: "How on earth do you spell that word?" He goes to dictionary to look up the spelling. In the fourth sentence, he stops in the middle: "I don't know the right word for what I want to say."

Scene 2: Smart Person Starts to Write

Smart Susan takes out the document plan (or outline) prepared earlier and puts it nearby. She pulls out paper (or keyboard) and starts writing about the first item. She commits the thoughts in her brain to the paper just as they occur. She does not stop to agonize over a word or a spelling or a fact; she simply writes down whatever she is thinking about a particular point. Then she moves on to the next point.

Remember, you cannot write and edit at the same time. Two entirely different brain processes will be warring with each

25

other, and only one will win. You will have to stop writing in order to edit (to search for just the right word, decide a phrase doesn't sound right, or whatever). And then you have lost your momentum.

It will probably feel strange at first, but this process really works: WRITE THE WHOLE THING FIRST! EDIT LATER!

WRITE WITHOUT STOPPING

Those who teach creative writing stress a technique called "free-writing." Essentially, it means "writing without stopping." Some professors go even further: "Don't even take the pen off the paper." The theory is that the act of writing—the physical process of moving pen across paper or fingers on keyboard activates the creative part of your mind. Even if you write "I can't think what to write, can't think what to write," you have engaged the appropriate brain cells, and the process of writing creates its own momentum.

Free-writing works well in the business world too. Take each major point, one at a time, and start writing. Commit to paper everything that passes through your mind about that one topic. Whatever words you're thinking, write those words down. Don't try to pass them through an editorial filter located somewhere between your brain and your fingers. Don't convert them into a more "businessy" style. Don't stop to evaluate what you've written; just keep writing.

The thing that keeps this process from being totally chaotic (and therefore unproductive) is that you have already done the "heavy" thinking of deciding what to include. If you follow your planned outline, taking each point in sequence, you can focus your thoughts, like a laser, on one particular area.

WORK DURING YOUR BEST HOURS

One way to make a difficult task easier is to work on it when you are at your best. If you are faced with a writing project that you dread, at least try to work on it when you are freshest.

This sounds very simple, but, unfortunately, it's human nature to put off a task we don't like. So what happens? You have to write a report for your boss, but you hate writing, so you procrastinate and suddenly it's the end of the day, when you are too tired to think clearly.

If you've never thought about which times of the day your energy level is high and when it is low, now is the time.

My highest energy hours are _____

My lowest energy hours are _____

CREATE A CONDUCIVE ENVIRONMENT

Does your working environment help you with the task of writing, or does it get in the way? For a short project, you don't need to be particularly concerned with this question. But the more crucial the piece you are writing, and the more difficult it seems to you, the more important it becomes to create an environment that helps, rather than hinders, the process.

Let's assume you're working on something that's important and difficult. Give yourself a break: Make your surroundings conducive to concentration. Here are some things you can do to keep your focus.

☑ Shut your office door.
☑ Don't permit telephone interruptions. Have someone take messages for you, or if that's not possible, unplug the darned thing.
☑ Clear your desk of everything else.
☑ Hide. Go to an empty office, the library, the storage room—anywhere people can't find you to interrupt you.
☑ Indulge in whatever tricks you need to get yourself

in a writing frame of mind: Sharpen the pencils, get out the special yellow pad, visualize the paper filled with words.

☑ Set a timer for a specific period—say, fifteen minutes. Write without stopping until the timer goes off. Then take a break. Then set your timer again.

DEALING WITH WRITER'S BLOCK

We are all vulnerable to writer's block: that awful feeling when the words just won't come. Writer's block isn't romantic, unless you're Somerset Maugham. In the business context, it's a nuisance and a problem that has to be overcome—fast. Here are some tricks.

- For each main point in your plan or outline, repeat this sentence to yourself: The main thing about _____ is that _____. This will give you a handle for leveraging the rest of that section. (Figure 4 contains some samples.)
- Imagine that the person you are writing to is sitting on the other side of your desk. She hears you say, "The main thing about _____ is that _____." She responds, "That's nice. Why should I care?" Pick up the conversation at that point and explain—in writing—why the item is important.
- Pretend you've been trying for weeks to get through to the governor of your state to talk about this issue, but have been blocked at every turn by his assistant's assistant. Finally you get through to the assistant: You have ten seconds to state your case.
- Write about the agony of writing. "Poor Carlos. He had to write a memo convincing his boss that the department needed another person during tax season, but he couldn't decide how to go about it. The blank paper stared at him accusingly. He didn't think he could do it. Where are the words? Then suddenly he realized . . ."

> To communicate, put your thoughts in order; give them a purpose; use them to persuade, to instruct, to discover, to seduce.
>
> —WILLIAM SAFIRE

(Text continues on page 30.)

Figure 4. An example of topics to consider when writer's block occurs.

Benefits

    The main thing about benefits is

    _____ .

Costs

    The main thing about costs is

    _____ .

Training Required

    The main thing about training is

    _____ .

Space Considerations

    The main thing about space is

    _____ .

Don't worry if what you have written seems too casual. Or too technical. Or too anything else. You're going to fix all that in the next phase.

Now set the draft aside. Try to arrange your schedule so that some period of time passes before you work on it again. That isn't always possible, of course; and for short documents it isn't always necessary. But if this writing project has a lot riding on it, you'll want to review it carefully. And you'll do a much better job of reviewing it if you can see it objectively, with fresh eyes.

CHAPTER 5

STEP 3:
POLISHING THE FIRST DRAFT

Now it is time to take your free-form writing and make it right. There is a great deal to check for.

- ☑ Tone
- ☑ Organization
- ☑ Style
- ☑ Correctness

IS THE TONE APPROPRIATE?

As a first step in the review process, read the entire draft quickly. Don't pay attention to details yet; just absorb the overall "feel" of the piece. Try to stand in the shoes of the person you are writing to. How would that person react to what you have written?

Tone has nothing to do with the value of the ideas in your document and everything to do with the emotional responses it triggers. It is probably the most subtle ingredient in written communications, and the most difficult for you to judge by yourself.

Ask someone who's not involved to read your draft and tell you his or her reaction. If you can't do that, at least wait overnight and read it fresh the next morning. Pretend you're seeing it for the first time. How does it affect you?

Problem: Defensive Tone Conveys Wrong Message

I am sorry for the frustration you have experienced during your conversion process. Premier Bank continues to service hundreds of clients throughout the United States and I am confident in our ability to provide competent professional administrative and recordkeeping service to your employees.

In other words, "We never make a mistake (even though we did this one time). Nobody else has complained."

Problem: Condescending Tone

I built this report to be used as a tool by you. Please verify it and pay attention to it.

Addressing your staff as if they were naughty schoolchildren is not the best way to build a strong team.

IS IT WELL ORGANIZED?

Now is the time to make sure your argument is well organized. You don't want readers to get lost, or to arrive at a conclusion prematurely.

Is the Logic Apparent? Is It Well Reasoned?

Because you invested the time during the planning phase to organize your points in a logical sequence, the overall structure of your presentation should be sturdy.

But it doesn't hurt to double-check at this point, especially if you're writing a major document. Here's a quick way to verify that your original scheme still makes sense.

Read each paragraph. On a separate sheet of paper, note in one or two words what that paragraph is about. When you're all done, you will have a chronological list of your points. Now study the list and evaluate the logic: Does your presentation take the reader where you want him to go, and in the most effective way?

Is the Purpose Obvious?

Nothing is more frustrating than trying to figure out what a document is all about. In the review stage, you must ensure that the core issue is immediately clear—and that means putting it in the first sentence, or at least the first paragraph.

In the planning stage you spent some time defining your purpose; your task now is to verify that you followed through and wrote it down clearly. This is harder than you might think: When you are intimately familiar with a situation, it's easy to forget that other people need a grounding rod.

Purpose Up Front: BEFORE	Purpose Up Front: AFTER
Enclosed for your information is the draft revision of the Data Security Manual for sections 2.1-3 and 2.3-2. Section 2.3-2 now differentiates between packaged and unpackaged tapes and data files in terms of the requirements for logging. This revision will be reviewed and must be approved by the Conference before it is official.	We are in the process of revising the Data Security Manual, and we would like your help with the section on receiving and logging tapes.

Is the Action Step Clearly Stated?

In your planning phase, you pinpointed the action step you desire, and planned where it should go in the document. Now, let's see if it's as clear as you think it is.

Problem: Action Step Not Clear

During the implementation of the Hawthorne Unit, several problems and construction-related issues were raised by operations. Many issues have been resolved, but there are a few that linger and need to be updated. If there are issues that are pending or have not been satisfactorily resolved, please contact me at extension 3176.

This is the opening paragraph of a two-page memo. The action step has been incorporated into the purpose statement, but neither is explicit enough to be useful. What is the reader being asked to do? The "please contact me" sentence is meaningless as an action step, for the writer already knows that some issues are still pending. When writing an action step, be specific, thorough, and tactful.

Action Step Clearly Articulated

We would like to discuss this proposal with the regional managers in a conference call on Monday, March 25 at 10:00 A.M. It would be helpful if you could fax your responses to the questions in this letter to all those participating by Friday, March 22. A list of the particpants is enclosed.

Does the Piece Flow Smoothly From Beginning to End?

Remember this sad truth: The person reading your document has little time. You stand a better chance of having your message understood if you lead your reader by the hand through the progression of ideas. One way to do this is with good transitions.

Transition words and phrases point readers in a certain direction. They function like highway signs, alerting readers to what lies ahead.

Here are some common transition words and phrases:

On the other hand,	Meanwhile
For example,	In fact,
Also,	Of course,
Similarly,	In other words,
However,	As a result,
In that case,	In general,
First,	Unfortunately,
Finally,	Luckily for us,
Most important,	Surprisingly,
Therefore,	Incidentally,
In sum,	Nevertheless,

There are many others, of course. As you review your draft, look for places where you switched course mentally but ne-

Modern writing at its worst consists in gumming together long strips of words which have already been set in order by someone else, and making the results presentable by sheer humbug. The

(continues)

attraction of this way of writing is that it is easy. It is easier— even quicker, once you have the habit—to say *In my opinion it is not an unjustifiable assumption that* than to say *I think.*

—GEORGE ORWELL

glected to verbally signal your change. As a general rule, transitions work best when they are at (or near) the beginning of the sentence.

A similar device for readers in a hurry is a pointer. To make sure readers don't overlook a key item, create a phrase that points to it. For example (the pointer phrases are in italics):

> "In almost all cases, our findings verified our original assumptions with *one major exception* . . ."
> "We believe this proposal offers *three main benefits* to the department: . . ." [then provide an enumerated list].
> "It has been a difficult process. But *this* we will never forget: . . ."
> "Working with customers from other countries and other cultures can present new challenges. *Here's* an example: . . ."

Each of those phrases operates like a little red flag or a whistle, saying, in effect, "Here comes something important."

WRITING STYLE: IS IT READABLE?

When CEOs say they look for people who know how to write, this is basically what they mean: people who can put together a sentence (and hence a whole document) that is clear, to the point, and unambiguous, with a little style and grace.

In the world of business writing, two monsters guard the gates of style: wordiness and passive constructions. If you can slay those two demons, you'll be well on your way.

Wordiness

You can't compensate for fuzzy thinking with excess words. Even when the idea is clear in your own mind, using too many words to express it will only suffocate it.

You are now going to go through your draft and take out all the unnecessary words. Be tough.

Problem: Wordiness

In 1990, we streamlined the job description form (copy attached). When writing a job description, remember it is not the quantity of information but the quality of the information that is important. The following are guidelines to keep in mind when writing a job description.

Solution: Tough Tightening

~~In 1990, we streamlined the job description form~~

~~(copy attached).~~ When writing a job description,

that quality

remember ~~it is not the quantity~~ of information ~~but~~

is more important than quantity.

~~the quality of the information that is important.~~ The

Keep these

~~following are~~ guidelines ~~to keep~~ in mind, ~~when writ-~~

~~ing a job description.~~

Problem: Wordiness

As such, there is a supposition that new techniques must be found to obtain valid information about the needs and hopes of the most needy in our community.

Solution: Simpler Sentences

~~As such, there is a supposition that new techniques~~

We need better ways to find out

~~must be found to obtain valid information about the~~

what the

~~needs and hopes of the~~ most needy in our commu-

nity *need and hope for.*

Would you like to try it? Here's an excerpt from the draft report of a quasi-governmental agency, circulated to solicit varying opinions. You have free range to edit.

Be on the lookout for phrases and sentences of which you are especially proud. This is nothing but your ego talking. Don't forget: You are not writing for yourself.

Passive Construction

No single thing you can do will improve your writing as much as eliminating the passive voice. The place to do it is in the editing phase.

Read over your composi- tions, and when you meet a passage which you think is particularly fine, strike it out.

—SAMUEL JOHNSON

DO-IT-YOURSELF QUIZ: WORDINESS

For any given amount of debt, lowering its associ-

ated interest rate and lengthening its repayment

term will reduce its periodic repayment burden. But

as most housing assets are financed over a rela-

tively long term—20 years or more—there is typi-

cally little significant progress that can be made

from additional extensions in the repayment hori-

zon.

Not sure what "passive voice" means? Think back to ninth-grade English classes, and recall the two main parts of a sentence: the subject and the verb. When the subject is *doing* the action of the verb, that sentence is in the *active voice*. When the subject is *receiving* the action of the verb, that sentence is in the *passive voice*.

Passive   The quarterly report was prepared by this department.

Active   This department [or "We"] prepared the quarterly report.

Passive   Determination of feasibility is desired and requested by the proposed sponsor, Barton Athletic Equipment, Inc.

Active   Barton Athletic Equipment, the proposed sponsor, requests determination of feasibility.

The word "by" is a dead giveaway to the passive voice; although sometimes it is implied rather than stated explicitly, as in this example:

Passive   The promotional guidelines, which allow up to an 8 percent increase for one or more grade levels, have been revised.

This statement illustrates one major reason why the passive is so popular in business: It lets the writer off the hook. You don't have to say who changed the promotion policy. The other reason it is so popular is more benign: sheer habit.

Why is passive bad? Because it is cowardly. Because it invariably results in a sentence that is longer than necessary. And most of all because it produces weak, wimpy sentences.

Try your hand at removing the passive voice.

Pompous Language

There is another flaw that almost all business writing is subject to: the automatic use of pompous, pretentious, old-fashioned, stuffy phrases.

DO-IT-YOURSELF QUIZ: PASSIVE VOICE

Upon our receiving the approved Form No. 3126 from your office, project processing will be continued.

_____

_____

_____

_____

"This is to acknowledge receipt of . . ."

"Per your request of April 29, . . ."

"Pursuant to our recent conversation, please be advised that . . ."

This kind of language is a carryover from the days of quill pens and foolscap; it simply has no place in the 1990s. And yet every day, all over the country, millions of people begin their correspondence with "Enclosed please find . . ."

It's time to break that habit. Near the back of this book, in the section called *Do's and Don'ts and Other Handy Resources*, you will find a list of the more egregious of these antiquated phrases. Use it as a template while you review your drafts.

DEVELOPING A LIVELY STYLE

After you have taken out the excess verbiage, "activated" the passive voice, and dumped the pompous language into the ashcan, what more can you do to your sentences to make them lively and interesting to read?

Vary Sentence Length

In general, shorter is better. Variation in sentence length is better still. Nothing contributes to boredom so much as sameness in length and rhythm. You don't want to be like John Dewey, the nineteenth-century educator, whose style was said to have "the monotonous consistency of peanut butter."

Varied Sentence Length

Establishing the bin for TRM tapes appears to eliminate the first problem (compliance with #2.3) but creates a new one (compliance with #2.2). We must be able to establish proof of delivery from couriers. How can this be done?

Use Strong, Courageous Words

Something compels us, when we start writing, to put in more and more words. There seems to be a sense that we add authority when we add words. So we take a strong verb like "investigate" and make it longer by writing "conduct an investigation," or if we really want to be impressive, we write "instigate an investigation." We can't just "testify," we have to "provide testimony." We have taken the verb and converted it into a noun. And in the process we have greatly weakened the impact of the sentence.

In the back of this book is a list of examples of verb conversion. It would be practically impossible to provide a complete list, since you can convert almost any verb; however, it is intended to make you aware of the problem.

Use Ordinary Words

Sometimes I think that at the front door of every office building in America is an invisible language screen. As people come through the door on their way to work in the morning, that screen filters out their ability to think in common English, so that all day long, whenever they need to write something, they must switch over to another language: corporatese.

On some occasions it is appropriate to write formally; however, it is never appropriate to write stuffed-shirt sentences.

Stuffy Sentence	Plain Sentence
We will advise you of our determination as soon as we review the requested documentation	After we have reviewed the material, we will let you know our decision.
It would seem to be incumbent upon your office to review these safety procedures and establish operational standards.	Since this falls within your area, we'd appreciate your help in drawing up the new safety standards.

A related problem is the use of jargon: the special vocabulary of a particular field or industry. It is perfectly acceptable to use jargon if everyone who is going to be reading your document speaks the language. In fact, it's often a mistake not to use it: You may seem like an outsider when you want to be perceived as a member of the group. But jargon is not appropriate if even one reader is unfamiliar with it. If you're uncertain, err on the side of plain English.

Use Humor

Go ahead—let a bit of your personality peek through. When the situation is appropriate, a light touch is wonderfully refreshing.

Lighten Up

I was correct the other day regarding the range and resolution numbers, just not confident. (After all, I was standing, not sitting.)

This E-mail excerpt is all the more charming since it comes from an electronics engineer, a profession usually thought to be bereft of all sense of humor.

Use Unusual Sentence Construction

Make your writing livelier by using an unusual construction once in a while.

☑ Ask a question, then answer it. Why? Because it commands attention.

☑ Interrupt yourself—to emphasize an idea—and then continue.

☑ Create parallel constructions: My challenge is to introduce you to the idea of parallelism; your challenge is to incorporate it judiciously in your writing.

☑ Deliberately repeat words for emphasis: Repetition is not necessarily bad; in fact, repetition is sometimes just what you need.

☑ Put the main point at the end—emphatically.

We can summarize this entire issue of writing style in a few rules:

- Write short sentences.
- Use the active voice.
- Use short words.
- Vary the length of your sentences.
- Put the action in the verb, not in the noun.
- Break some rules—carefully.

> **The most valuable of all talents is that of never using two words when one will do.**
>
> **—THOMAS JEFFERSON**

IS IT MECHANICALLY CORRECT?

The very last thing to check for in your draft is that you have made no serious errors in punctuation, spelling, grammar, usage, or syntax. You need to find these errors and remove them. They create both a bad impression and a major distraction. At best, they cause your reader to stumble briefly and lose track of your point. At worst, they seriously damage your credibility.

Grammar

Most of the time, native speakers of the English language use correct grammar automatically. However, there are a few mistakes that show up often enough in written language that you should be on the lookout for them.

- Subject-verb disagreement

  Wrong: Deciding on specific strategies to improve safety conditions require considerable planning.

  Right: Deciding . . . requires considerable planning.

- Dangling modifiers

  Wrong: Writing to the entire staff, the president's report announced anticipated layoffs. [The report didn't do the writing.]

  Right: Writing to the entire staff, the president announced the anticipated layoffs.

Punctuation

Most of us have a bad attitude about punctuation, so let's put it in perspective: In the grand scheme of things, punctuation is less important than logical organization and clear wording. Still, you want to avoid truly horrible mistakes.

Nine times out of ten, you will get the punctuation right if you remember that it substitutes for vocal inflections and gestures that clarify meaning when we speak. A comma is the written equivalent of a pause; a semicolon is the written equivalent of a longer pause; an exclamation mark is the equivalent of shouting; a dash is the equivalent of stopping abruptly midsentence.

For a full rundown on punctuation, consult any good grammar reference. Here we are concerned only with a few common errors.

Comma: *Add a comma after introductory phrases.* If you would naturally pause when reading the sentence aloud, then a comma is appropriate.

Add a comma if confusion would otherwise result. To review, commas are sometimes needed in short sentences.

Semicolon: *Use a semicolon to separate two independent clauses (each could stand on its own as a full sentence).* The common mistake here is to use a comma instead; that creates what is known as a run-on sentence.

Dash: *Use a dash to indicate an abrupt stop.* Whenever we're chatting with a co-worker—and we all do it—we can use tonal inflection to show a detour of thought. In writing, we use dashes for that purpose, and also for another—punch.

Word Usage

Errors in usage are more serious: They make you look ignorant, and thus jeopardize your credibility. Unfortunately, it is easy to make usage mistakes: The English language is full of words that are easily confused with other words. Some are more distressing than others. Few people will think ill of you if you write "continuous" when you mean "continual," but if you write "accept" when you mean "except," they will think you sloppy—or worse. Some confusions completely change the meaning of the sentence: If you think people can deduce your meaning, that's an allusion.

In the final section of this book you will find a list of "lookalike" words that are commonly confused or misused. Read it over now and mark those that you have particular difficulty with. Whenever you are polishing a draft, be sure to look out for them.

Spelling

You *must* spell every word correctly. There is no excuse for anything less, and nothing more clearly brands you as incompetent than incorrect spelling. If you don't know how to spell something, look it up. If you have even the tiniest doubt, look it up.

"But I use a computer," you say; "the spell checker will take care of that." Maybe; maybe not. The hardest problem with spelling is the "lookalike" words: *stationery* and *stationary*;

capital and *capitol*. Spell checkers can't discriminate; the computer sees only a word that is spelled correctly.

One of the smartest men I know consistently writes "their" when he means "there." He's a highly educated engineer who designs circuits that are used in the space shuttle, but because of simple errors, his memos are difficult to take seriously.

You will find spelling help at the end of this book: words that are often spelled incorrectly, and lookalike words that are often mixed up.

CHAPTER 6

STEP 4: FORMATTING FOR EASY READING

A great many people think that polysyllables are a sign of intelligence.

—BARBARA WALTERS

You've analyzed your reader, focused your purpose, brainstormed your ideas, planned your strategy, and polished your text until it shines. But your document could still be a failure, for a reason that's so obvious it's easy to overlook: No one will read it.

Don't forget, this business of writing is all about time—something that the people who pick up your letter or memo are most likely profoundly short of. They are already overwhelmed by the sheer volume of written material that comes their way. You must grab their attention in the first few seconds. It's partly a function of the first sentence or first paragraph, but on a more visceral level it is not a function of the words at all, but of what the page itself looks like. Is it inviting and easy to read, or an overwhelming avalanche of words?

Your proposal is sitting on your manager's desk, along with a number of other pieces. At the end of a tough day, she finally has a chance to tackle her in-box. Will she read your piece, or will she set it aside and move on to the next one?

That decision is made within seconds, and it is usually a subconscious reaction to the overall look of the document. If the piece looks daunting, the reader will move on to something that appears more manageable. Take a look at the page reproduced in Figure 5: It's *one* page from a four-page memo. Would you want to read it?

In the final analysis, then, your success as a writer could depend on how you choose to format the piece on the page (or screen,

Figure 5.   A page from a four-page memo.

next business day for trades executed via voice response system. A
significant advantage according to IDS is the real time accounting/
investment management, which provides administrators without the need to
explain earnings allocations.

Critics regarding daily valuation note that it's expensive, it's
unnecessary, employees don't use it, and it potentially leads to abuse.

IDS provides telephone transfer capabilities. Less than 15% of 1-800 calls
received in a given timeframe were transfer requests of existing dollars.
IDS reports that the significant majority of calls are to inquire as to
account balances and investment performance.

A significant and critical issue regarding daily valuation presents itself
in terms of education of participants. Daily valuation implies that a
participant may trade assets on a daily basis and in essence "manage" their
investments. Education wil be a critical role for sponsors. They must
provide employees with tools to manage their dollars, and converting to
daily accounting alone won't do this.

Additionally, others have noted that daily valuation leads to a short-term
orientation for participants. This runs counter to the entire premise of
these retirement plans in that the investment is for the long term. Given
that this is a long-term investment, daily valuation and access to these
funds may run contrary to the ultimate desired result of asset accumulation.

There is some question as to whether or not daily valuation encourages
participants to borrow funds or transfer funds at will. Limited historical
data seem to suggest that it in fact does not. T. Rowe Price looked at a
number of plans with daily valuation services, which encompassed 200,000
participants. Using the 1-800 telephone service, they average .6 calls per
participant per year. Of these, less than 2/10 of one percent were
transactions requested by a participant per year. Most calls are purely of
the inquiry-only nature.

A Febuary 18, 1991, edition of Pensions and Investments notes that
recordkeeping firms are scrambling to attract new clients, and that
competition is fierce. The article notes that mutual fund institutions have
made great gains on the business, largely due to their pre-existing data
processing capabilities. Note that these capabilities are specifically
daily valued systems.

Many mutual fund managers, such as Frank Russel Company, have now joined
others by offering "one-stop shopping." Russell is now selling
recordkeeping services as an enticement to the firm's mutual fund offering
with the communication advantages of daily valuation offered via telephone
to participants.

It seems to me that our challenge is to be in a position to provide the same
or greater capabilities should our clients be willing to purchase them.
While we know that certainly not all clients will require this level of
service, it seems abundantly clear that this is the direction in which the
industry is migrating. In fact, some providers are already there, and we
have felt the brunt of their lead on us in terms of plan service.

for electronic mail). Once the recipient begins reading, all the other ingredients of good writing—style, clarity, logical organization, readability—become important. But first you have to get them to read it.

After you have finished reviewing your draft and are satisfied with the text, you are ready for the final step: Go through the entire piece and look for places where you can add visual interest. Four main devices are:

1. Short paragraphs
2. Headings
3. Lists
4. Graphics: charts, tables, figures

The surest way to make your document reader-friendly is to incorporate lots of white space. In addition to substantive value, each of these four techniques contributes white space to your document, making the finished piece easy on the eye.

SHORT PARAGRAPHS

Somewhere along the line you've probably learned this rule about paragraphs: Change paragraphs whenever you change ideas. It's a good rule, as far as it goes, but it's often difficult to apply. Suppose you have one main idea and three examples: Do you write one paragraph or four? Suppose your main point is supported by two secondary facts: Do you put them all together into one paragraph or separate them?

In paragraphs, less is more. Even if three points are very clearly linked together under one main idea, make separate paragraphs. Group them under a heading (see next section) if you need to demonstrate their relationship to each other. No one will get lost reading three very short paragraphs in sequence, especially if you take care to use good transition words. But there is a good chance of losing the thread in a very long paragraph, even if the multiple points fall under one main idea.

Problem: Long Paragraphs Are Hard to Read Quickly

Difference Account balances are transferred to Current expense on a monthly basis. The home accounting office has taken over the function of moving these balances as part of the centralization of branch accounting. All Difference Account balances for each regional office will be moved in Late General Ledger processing as of the 25th of each month (or the previous work day if the 25th is a weekend or holiday). Any balance that is in a Difference Account at the close of business on the 25th will be transferred early the next morning in Late General Ledger before the books for the 25th are final. Your accounting proof for the 25th will contain the balances prior to the transfer.

Solution: Break Into Smaller Paragraphs

Difference Account balances are transferred to Current expense on a monthly basis. The home accounting office has taken over the function of moving these balances as part of the centralization of branch accounting.

All Difference Account balances for each regional office will be moved in Late General Ledger processing as of the 25th of each month (or the previous work day if the 25th is a weekend or holiday).

Any balance that is in a Difference Account at the close of business on the 25th will be transferred early the next morning in Late General Ledge before the books for the 25th are final.

Your accounting proof for the 25th will contain the balances prior to the transfer.

Can a paragraph be too short? Nope. Look at this very effective letter. How long is the first paragraph? Does it get your attention?

The Power of Short Paragraphs

Oops!

You recently received a message on your billing statement that read "A $20 annual membership fee may appear on your next monthly statement."

Please disregard this message. It was printed in

error. YOU WILL NOT BE CHARGED AN AN-
NUAL MEMBERSHIP FEE NEXT MONTH.

We apologize for any confusion or inconvenience
this may have caused you.

The writer of this memo used another trick—all caps—to make
sure the single most important point is not overlooked.

HEADINGS

Headings function like tour guides. They lead your readers
through the sequence of ideas, all the while announcing what's
coming: "Next we are going to be visiting a new topic: cost/
benefit analysis." They ensure that no one gets lost, and serve
as sign markers if someone wants to return later and study
something more closely.

The headings in your document will closely reflect the main
topics in your outline plan; in fact, the headings may *be* the
topics. However, they'll be more effective as headings if you
strive to make them more than mere labels.

Flat heading:	Costs of Proposed System
Attention-getting:	How Much Will It Cost?
Flat Heading:	Section 503: Sick Leave
Attention-getting:	Sick Leave Is Expanded
Flat Heading:	Advertising and Marketing
Attention-getting:	New Advertising Ideas

Lengthy documents will probably benefit from two or more
levels of headings: main headings and subheadings, perhaps
even sub-subheadings if information is densely packed or de-
tailed. The outline you used to shape your document is a good
guide here: If a main idea has several supporting ideas, subheads
will help.

When working with subheads, be aware of the difference in
typographic presentation. Make sure that subheads of the same

level are typed the same way throughout, and that the physical format echoes the relationship of subordination.

ALL CAPS

are visually more important than
<u>Upper and Lower Case Underlined</u>

which is more important than

Upper and Lower Case

without underlining

If you have a word-processing system and a printer that permit the use of different type fonts, you have even more options for distinguishing between subheads. But exercise moderation: Use no more than two typefaces (one for headings, one for text), or stick to just one typeface and use three variations: bold, italic, and regular. More than that and you have created an unreadable jumble.

For longer documents, headings are crucial. However, they can be helpful even for shorter pieces. Keep this firmly in mind: The reader of the document is pressed for time. Anything you can do to shorten the reading and understanding time is a valuable investment.

Let's look at a typical one-page memo. (You're right—it's also typically wordy, but that's not our concern at the moment.)

Memos just don't move the heart and the soul.

—ERVIN SHAMOS

LISTS

An effective way to highlight information is to present it in list format. Listed items are usually indented (which is a good highlight technique by itself), and they usually have some marking device (either a number or a symbol). The result is that they practically jump off the page.

As you review your draft, be on the lookout for sentences that could be presented in the form of a list. If you have a sentence that contains items separated with (a) numbers or (b) letters, it is an obvious candidate for a listing. But even if they don't

(*Text continues on page 54.*)

MEMO WITHOUT HEADINGS

Attached are the Department Batch Header form and timesheets that were generated by the Time Reporting System for the August 16–31 pay cycle. Timesheets are generated only for employees who have exceptions to their regular semimonthly pay. If there were no employees in your department with exceptions, you will only find a Department Batch Header form attached.

Please verify the timesheets by adding the totals of each category on the individual timesheets and comparing the results to the totals listed on the Department Batch Header form. If you find a discrepancy, please contact either Sally Smith or Mary McGregor.

Individual timesheets must be signed by the employee and by department management. Please make every effort to have employees sign their timesheets. If an employee is unavailable for signature, make a notation and Personnel will be responsible for obtaining the employee's signature at a later date.

The Department Batch Header form must be signed by the department manager and the officer if there are timesheets with exceptions. If there are no exceptions, only the department manager needs to sign the Department Batch Header form.

Timesheets and Batch Header forms must be returned to Personnel no later than 2:00 P.M. on September 4. If you have any questions, please do not hesitate to call either Sally Smith or Mary McGregor.

SAME MEMO WITH HEADINGS

Payroll Information for Your Staff

Attached are the Department Batch Header form and timesheets that were generated by the Time Reporting System for the August 16–31 pay cycle.

Timesheets are generated only for employees who have exceptions to their regular semimonthly pay. If there were no employees in your department with exceptions, you will only find a Department Batch Header form attached.

Timesheets

Please verify the timesheets by adding the totals of each category on the individual timesheets and comparing the results to the totals listed on the Department Batch Header form. If you find a discrepancy, please contact either Sally Smith or Mary McGregor.

Individual timesheets must be signed by the employee and by department management. Please make every effort to have employees sign their timesheets. If an employee is unavailable for signature, make a notation and Personnel will be responsible for obtaining the employee's signature at a later date.

Batch Header

The Department Batch Header form must be signed by the department manager and the officer if there are timesheets with exceptions. If there are no exceptions, only the department manager needs to sign the Department Batch Header form.

Your Deadline

Timesheets and Batch Header forms must be returned to Personnel no later than 2:00 P.M. on September 4. If you have any questions, please do not hesitate to call either Sally Smith or Mary McGregor.

contain any itemization, sentences can often be restructured so that you can use the list format.

Lists can be constructed using some kind of symbol or using numbers. Printers with type fonts offer many symbols:

☐ Item	■ Item	● Item
☐ Item	■ Item	● Item
☐ Item	■ Item	● Item

However, several characters on regular typewriters work just as well:

* Item	– Item	–/ Item
* Item	– Item	–/ Item
* Item	– Item	–/ Item

Numbered lists work well when you are describing something where the sequence is significant (a repair procedure, for instance), or where the sentence that leads into the list mentions a number. For example:

> We believe the new system offers three significant advantages:
>
> 1. It is easier to train operators to use it.
> 2. It has been proved much more reliable, so downtime is considerably reduced.
> 3. The output is easier to read.

Problem: Information Is Hard to Find

As a result of these efforts, we are pleased to announce the opening of four new sales offices. The office locations are as follows: Boston, Philadelphia, Seattle, and Tucson. The managers of new offices are Amanda Baker, Charles Davis, Ed Fortunata, and George Halbertson, respectively.

Solution: Create a List

As a result of these efforts, we are pleased to announce the opening of four new sales offices:

Location	Manager
Boston	Amanda Baker
Philadelphia	Charles Davis
Seattle	Ed Fortunata
Tucson	George Halbertson

SAD BUT TRUE

The person who receives your document will decide in approximately four seconds whether to read what took you hours, perhaps days, to write.

GRAPHICS

Technically, the list of the four new offices is a table: two parallel lists, each with a heading. Tables, charts, diagrams, figures—all kinds of graphics are very effective ways to add white space to your document and present information in such a way that it can be quickly grasped.

Effective Use of Tables

Effective January 1, 1990, the company revised its guidelines for salary increases. The following guidelines are now in effect:

Promotion	Policy	Suggested Guideline
One grade	0–8% or minimum of new grade	6–8%
Two grades	0–15% or minimum of new grade	10–12%
Three grades	0–15% or minimum of new grade	12–15%

Most of the document software packages used in large organizations have the capability for producing charts and graphs or some other kind of visual. This section is not intended to demonstrate how to create graphics, but to remind you to keep them in mind. Your task here, in the polishing phase, is to critically evaluate your document and make sure you don't overlook any opportunities to lighten up the look of the finished piece.

As an example, a manager in the human resources department of a large organization needed to let everyone know that some of the people in his group had moved to new offices. He chose to present this information in a series of one-sentence paragraphs:

> Carolyn Miller is now in the Credit Section, next to the receptionist's desks, to the left of the blueprint machine.

> Bill Koenig and Chris Samuels will be located in the former Building Security area, just inside the glass wall.

And so on . . . for a page and a half. This is the sort of information that lends itself to graphics. Even a hand-drawn map would communicate the message better than this series of verbal descriptions that readers have to mentally translate into pictures.

The visual appeal of your document is vital. It's the last step, but it's the first thing the reader will notice. With the graphics capability available in so many common software programs, you should find this an easy chore—maybe even fun.

CHAPTER 7

A WRITER'S CHECKLIST

Reading
maketh a
full man;
conference
a ready
man; and
writing an
exact man.

—FRANCIS
BACON

STEP 1: PLANNING YOUR WRITING

☐ Do I need to write this? Would a phone call work better? A meeting?

☐ Do I know why I'm writing this? Have I clearly articulated to myself exactly what I want to have happen when this piece is read?

☐ Do I know who's the primary audience?

☐ Is there a possibility others may read it in the future?

☐ Have I taken the time to analyze my audience? Have I considered:

—How much about the situation do they already know?

—How much technical background in the field do they have?

—Do they already have an opinion about this situation?

—What do I know about them that might color their reaction? Their personality? Their experience with similar problems in the past? Their particular pet peeves?

☐ Have I figured out what kind of document I should write? Memo? Letter? Summary overview? Full background report? Brief request? Full-fledged proposal?

☐ Do I know exactly what I want the recipient to do as a next step?

☐ Considering what this is about and whom it is being sent to, do I know what tone would be most appropriate? Can I state in one word what tone I am going to strive for in the finished document?

☐ Have I included all the information I need? Have I forgotten anything? Have I taken out all the things I don't need?

☐ Where am I going to put the action step?

☐ Is there a place for the statement of purpose?

STEP 2: WRITING THE FIRST DRAFT

☐ Have I scheduled this writing job for my best hours? Or am I trying to write this when I'm already exhausted?

☐ Have I done everything I can to make the physical environment appropriate for writing?
—Shut the door? Work in another office?
—Block telephone interruptions?
—Collect the necessary information and get rid of everything else on the desk?

☐ Do I remember what this phase is all about: writing, not critiquing?

STEP 3: POLISHING THE FIRST DRAFT

☐ Am I sure the tone is what I intended? If I'm not sure, can I get someone to read it for me?

☐ Is the organization right? When I read straight through without stopping, does the conclusion seem logical?

☐ Do the important points stand out?

☐ Is the purpose obvious in the first paragraph? Is it clearly and succinctly phrased? Could someone get it in a second or two?

☐ Is the action step clear and explicit? Is it in an obvious place?

☐ Do the ideas flow smoothly?

☐ Have I used good transitions?

☐ Is the writing unnecessarily wordy? Have I taken a hard, critical look at each and every word in the sentence?

☐ Are there pet sentences that I am especially proud of? Do I have the courage to take them out?

☐ Have I reworded every passive construction into the active voice?

☐ Have I avoided stuffy language as much as possible?

☐ Have I matched up my sentences against the list of antiquated phrases and gotten rid of all the pompous language?

☐ Do I have many more short sentences than long ones?

☐ Are the sentences of varying lengths?

☐ Have I used strong verbs and resisted the temptation to convert them into weak nouns?

☐ Have I found all the impressive-sounding words and replaced them with simple words?

☐ If I've added a little humor, is it appropriate here?

☐ Have I taken advantage of unusual structure occasionally—using questions, parallelism, repetition for emphasis?

☐ Are there any grammatical errors? If I think my grammar is weak, have I checked with a reference book?

☐ Is the punctuation correct—or at least not horribly incorrect? If I read the sentence aloud, would the punctuation marks echo my voice inflection?

☐ Have I used the right word? Have I checked the list of lookalike words for the ones I know I tend to confuse?

☐ Is every single word spelled correctly?

STEP 4: FORMATTING FOR EASY READING

☐ If I received my letter (or memo) in the mail, would I want to read it? Or is it so chock-full of WORDS that it looks like too much work to read?

☐ Have I divided long paragraphs into shorter ones?

☐ Are there enough headings to guide my reader through the document?

☐ If I used main headings and subheadings, are they typed appropriately?

☐ Did I find a way to word the headings so that they will engage the reader's attention?

☐ Have I made full use of lists?

☐ With lists, do I know when to use symbols and when to use numbers?

☐ Does the list contain only items that are parallel, that are like one another?

☐ Have I looked for places where I can create a table with two or more columns of information?

☐ Should I include some kind of graphic? Have I presented information visually whenever possible?

CHAPTER 8

DO'S AND DON'TS
AND OTHER HANDY RESOURCES

In this section you will find fingertip guides to some of the most common problems in business writing:

- How is that word spelled?
- Is this the right word? Or have I confused it with another?
- How can I say this in plain English?

DO'S AND DON'TS

Avoid	Use Instead
9 A.M. in the morning	9 A.M.
a long period of time	a long time
absolutely complete	complete
accorded	given
accounted for by the fact that	caused by
accrue	add, gain
achieve purification	purify
add the point that	add that
adequate enough	adequate
adjacent to	next to
advance forward	advance
advance warning	warning
advance planning	planning
adversely impact on	hurt, set back

Avoid	Use Instead
advised and informed	told, outlined
afford an opportunity	allow, let
an example of this is the fact that	for example
anxious and eager	anxious or eager
are of the opinion that	believe that
ascertain	find, learn
assembled together	assembled
at this point in time	now
attach together	attach
basic fundamentals	fundamentals
be in possession of	have
brief in duration	brief
call your attention to the fact that	remind you
circular in shape	circular
circulate around	circulate
close proximity	near
commence	begin
consensus of opinion	consensus
consequent results	results
continue to remain	remain
cooperate together	cooperate
desire	want
despite the fact that	although, though
due to the fact that	because
during the course of	during
effectuate the policy	carry out the policy
end result	result
endeavor	try
evidenced	showed
exactly identical	identical
expertise	ability, skill
facilitate	help
final completion	completion

Avoid	Use Instead
following after	after
for the reason that	since, because
had occasion to be	was
have need for	need
immediately and at once	immediately or at once
impacted	affected, changed
in accordance with	by, following
in order to	to
in the event that	if
in the near future	soon
in view of the fact that	since, because
initiate	begin
interpose no objection	don't object
is comprised of	is composed of, comprises
it is interesting to note that	(don't use; just make your point)
mutual cooperation	cooperation
neat in appearance	neat
necessary requisite	requisite
never before in the past	never before
on the order of	about
owing to the fact that	since, because
pertaining to	of, about
prior to	before
recall back	recall
recur again	recur
reduce down	reduce
refer back to	refer
reiterate again	reiterate, restate, repeat
repeat again	repeat
report back	report
reside	live
resultant effect	effect
subsequent to	after
sufficient	enough

Avoid	Use Instead
the reason is because	because
time period	time
true facts	facts
ultimate end	end
utilize	use
very unique	unique
with the result that	so that

ANTIQUATED WORDS AND PHRASES

Avoid	Use Instead
above-mentioned	this, that
affix signature to	sign
aforementioned, aforesaid	this, that
aforementioned letter	the letter
answer is in the affirmative	answer is yes
appreciate your prompt compliance with	please do this as promptly as you can
as of this date	today
as of this writing	now
as per	according to
as per your request	as you requested
as regards	concerning, regarding
as stated above, as indicated below	as we have shown
at a later date	later
at an early date	soon
at once and by return mail	at once, immediately
at the earliest possible moment	soon (or give the date)
at the present writing	now
at this writing	now
at your earliest convenience	as soon as you can, by (date)

Avoid	Use Instead
attached hereto, herewith	attached is, we have attached
attached please find	you will find attached; I have included; here is
beg to inform you	think you should know
by return mail	soon, quickly
contact you by telephone	call you
deem	think
enclose my check in the amount of	enclose my check for
enclosed herewith	enclosed
enclosed please find	here is; we are sending
for the purpose of	for, to
have at hand	have
have duly noted the contents of	have read
heretofore	until now
hoping for the favor of a reply	we look forward to your reply
I am in receipt of your letter	I have your letter
if you require	if you need
in accordance with our request	as we have requested
in a timely manner	on time, promptly
in the amount of	for
in the event that	if
in re	regarding, concerning, about
in the near future	soon
in the matter of	about
is in consonance with	agrees with, follows
it has been brought to my attention	I have learned
it is incumbent upon us	we must
of recent date	of (the specific date)
pending receipt of	until we receive

Avoid	**Use Instead**
per your request	as you asked
permit me to say	(just say it)
permit me to take this opportunity to	I want to
pertaining to	about, of, on
please do not hesitate to	please
please enclose your remittance	please send your payment
pursuant to our recent conversation	as we discussed
pursuant to your request	as you asked
receipt is acknowledged	we received
replying to yours of	(be specific or omit)
said (e.g., "said amount")	the, this, that
subsequent to	after
thank you for your attention to this matter	please let us hear from you soon
thanking you in advance	thanks for your help
the favor of a reply is requested	(omit altogether)
the undersigned	I
the writer	I, me
this is to acknowledge receipt of	thank you for
this office	we, us
trusting you will	I hope, will you, won't you
under date of	explicit date
under separate cover	separately
until such time as	until
up to the present writing	up to now
upon that date	then
waiting your favor	please let us hear from you
we acknowledge receipt of	we have received
we are in receipt of your letter dated	we received your letter of

Avoid	Use Instead
we await your favor	please let us know
we have shipped same	we have shipped it
we herewith hand you our check	we enclose our check
we wish to say	(just say it)
with reference to	about
yours of recent date	your recent letter
yours of the 25th	your letter

And that all-time favorite:

"If I can be of any further assistance, please do not hesitate to call me."

Instead try something like this:

"I hope this helped. Please call if you need more information."

CONVERTED VERBS

Weak	Strong
achieve improvements	improve
are found to be in agreement	agree
begin implementation	implement
carry on the work of developing	develop
come to conclusions	conclude
engage in a confrontation	confront
exhibit a tendency to	tend to
get an evaluation	evaluate
give an estimate	estimate
give an indication of	indicate
give a weakness to	weaken
give assistance to	assist
give consideration to	consider

Weak	Strong
give proof of	prove
have a preference for	prefer
have discussions	discuss
institute an improvement in	improve
interpose an objection	object
is applicable	applies
is corrective of	corrects
is indicative of	indicates
is suggestive of	suggests
it is our conclusion as a result of our investigation	our investigation leads us to believe
it is our realization that	we realize
it would not be unreasonable to assume	I (we) assume
make a determination	determine
make a decision to	decide to
make a study of	study
make an adjustment to	adjust
make an approximation of	approximate
make an authorization	authorize
make an examination of	examine
make an exception to	except
make application to	apply
make declarations	declare
make mention of	mention
make out a list	list
make revisions	revise
make the acquaintance of	meet
make use of	use
obtain an increase in	increase
perform an analysis of	analyze
send the transmittal	transmit
show an illustration	illustrate

Weak	Strong
take action	act
take cognizance of	note
take into consideration	consider
undertake studies	study
write the documentation	document

"LOOKALIKE" WORDS THAT CAUSE SPELLING AND USAGE PROBLEMS

Word	Meaning or Part of Speech
accede	to agree
exceed	to go beyond
accent	speech coloration
ascent	the rise upward
assent	agreement
accept	to take
except	not including
access	entrance
excess	too much
adapt	to change
adept	facile
adopt	to take on
addition	arithmetic
edition	version of a publication
adverse	negative
averse	disinclined
advice	helpful suggestions (a noun)
advise	to give advice (a verb)
affect	a verb: to have impact on
effect	as a noun: the result; as a verb: to bring about
all ready	everything is ready
already	in the past
all together	everyone is together
altogether	completely

Word	Meaning or Part of Speech
allude	to make a reference to
elude	to escape
allusion	reference
illusion	mirage
altar	a place of worship
alter	to make a change in
appraise	to decide the value of
apprise	to inform
assure	to convince; to inform positively
ensure	to make certain that
insure	to take precaution against (as with insurance)
belief	a noun
believe	a verb
breadth	width
breath	inhalation (the noun)
breathe	to inhale (the verb)
canvas	a fabric
canvass	to take a poll
capital	the main city
capitol	the actual building
choose	present tense
chose	past tense
cite	to specify, to make reference to
sight	vision, or something seen
site	a spot you have decided upon
clothes	clothing, your wardrobe
cloths	individual pieces of fabric (like washcloths)
complement	to fit together with, to make up a whole
compliment	praise, to praise

Word	Meaning or Part of Speech
conscience	the inner voice that tells you what to do
conscious	awake, aware
continuous	without ever stopping
continual	continues indefinitely, but with pauses
copyright	registration of a book
copywriter	a person who writes advertising copy
council	a group of people
counsel	to give advice (or the advice given or the person who gives the advice)
consul	an official of a foreign government
detract	to take away from, to diminish
distract	to interrupt, to cause someone's attention to shift
discreet	tactful
discrete	completely separate
disinterested	unbiased, neutral
uninterested	not interested, bored
eminent	famous
imminent	about to happen soon
envelop	a verb: to encircle
envelope	a noun: that which holds a letter
forego	to come first
forgo	to do without
foreword	the preface of a book
forward	as a verb: to send on to someone else
	as an adjective or adverb: toward the front

Word	**Meaning or Part of Speech**
formally	in a formal manner
formerly	in the past
imply	to suggest (the speaker implies)
infer	to draw a conclusion (the listener infers)
incite	to stir up
insight	understanding, wisdom
it's	it is (It's hot today.)
its	belongs to "it" (Its destination was unknown.)
lead	as a noun: the metal as a verb: the present tense
led	past tense of verb "to lead"
lightening	becoming lighter
lightning	what goes with thunder
loose	not tight
lose	the verb
moral	the point to be learned from a fable; something that is inherently right
morale	psychological well-being
ordinance	rule or law
ordnance	weaponry
persecute	to torment
prosecute	to bring to trial
personal	always an adjective: private, or related to some person
personnel	a noun: a group of employees (sometimes adjective, as in "Personnel Department")

Word	Meaning or Part of Speech
precede	to go before in time, to occur at some earlier time
proceed	to continue, to go ahead
principal	as a noun: the money you borrowed, or the head of a school or a company as an adjective: main, primary
principle	always a noun: a strong belief
prophecy	a noun
prophesy	the verb
quiet	silent
quit	to stop
quite	very
respectfully	with respect
respectively	in the order named
stationary	not moving
stationery	writing paper
succeed	to do well
secede	to resign from a government structure
their	belongs to them
there	at that spot
they're	they are
thorough	complete, comprehensive
through	finished
you're	you are
your	belongs to you

BUSINESS WORDS FREQUENTLY MISSPELLED

abbreviate	accessory	accompanying
absence	accidentally	accordance
accessible	accommodate	accrued

accumulate
accuracy
achieve
acknowledge
acknowledgment
acquire
addendum
address
adjourn
adjustment
admissible
advantageous
advertisement
advisable
align
all right
allege
allotment
allotted
ambitious
amendment
analysis
analyze
announcement
annoyance
annual
anonymous
anxious
apologize
apparatus
apparent
applicable
applicant
appointment
appraisal
appropriate
approximate
ascertain
assessment
assignment
assistance

assistant
associate
authoritative
authorize
auxiliary
bankruptcy
bargain
beneficial
beneficiary
benefit
bookkeeper
brochure
budget
bulletin
business
calendar
caliber
campaign
cancellation
cannot
casually
catalog
category
cease
ceiling
certain
changeable
characteristic
chargeable
chiefly
choice
circumstances
client
clientele
collateral
commission
commitment
committed
committee
commodities
comparable

comparative
competence
competent
competitive
competitor
compromise
concede
conceivable
conceive
concession
concurred
conference
conferred
confidential
congratulate
consensus
consequence
consignment
consistent
conspicuous
controlling
controversial
controversy
convenience
convenient
cooperate
coordinate
cordially
correctable
correlation
correspondence
corroborate
creditor
criticism
criticize
currency
current
customary
customer
cylinder
dealt

debtor	emergency	expenditure
deceive	emphasis	expense
decision	emphasize	experience
deductible	employee	explanation
defense	enclose	extension
deferred	encouragement	extraordinary
deficient	endeavor	extremely
deficit	endorsement	facilities
definite	enforceable	familiar
definitely	enterprise	familiarize
definition	enthusiasm	favorable
delegate	entrust	favorite
dependent	environment	feasibility
depositors	equally	feasible
describe	equipment	February
description	equipped	financial
desirable	equitable	fiscal
desperate	equivalent	flexible
development	erratic	fluorescent
device	erroneous	focused
dilemma	especially	foreign
director	essence	forfeit
disappear	essential	formula
disappearance	eventually	fortunate
disappoint	evident	forty
disastrous	exaggerate	fourth
discernible	excellence	freight
discrepancy	excellent	frequently
dismissal	excerpt	fulfill
dissatisfied	excessive	fulfillment
division	exchangeable	fundamental
dominant	exclusively	furthermore
echelon	excusable	gauge
economical	exemption	generally
efficiency	exercise	genuine
efficient	exhaust	grateful
eighth	exhibition	grievance
either	existence	grievous
eligible	existent	guarantee
eliminate	exorbitant	guess
embarrass	expedite	guidance

handicapped	insurable	maneuver
handled	intelligence	manufacturer
harass	intention	maximum
hardware	intercede	meant
hazard	intercession	measurable
hazardous	interest	medal
headache	interfere	medicine
height	interrupted	mediocre
helpful	inventory	memorandum
hesitant	investor	merchandise
hierarchy	irregular	mileage
hindrance	irrelevant	miniature
humorous	itemized	minimum
identical	itinerary	minuscule
illegal	judgment	miscellaneous
illegible	juncture	misinterpreted
illicit	justifiable	modernize
immaterial	keypunch	monopoly
immediately	knowledge	monotonous
impatient	knowledgeable	morale
imperative	laboratory	mortgage
implement	latter	municipal
inaccessible	legible	naturally
inaccuracy	legitimate	necessary
inasmuch	leisure	necessitate
inasmuch as	letterhead	necessity
inaugurate	leveling	negligence
incidentally	liaison	negligent
incomparable	library	negligible
inconvenience	license	negotiable
incurred	licensee	negotiate
indebtedness	licensor	neighbor
independent	likelihood	nevertheless
indispensable	linear	nickel
individual	losing	niece
inducement	luncheon	noticeable
influential	magazine	notwithstanding
inherent	maintenance	nucleus
inquiry	manageable	nuisance
insignificant	management	numerous
installment	mandatory	oblige

obsolescence	permitted	promissory
obsolete	permitting	prototype
occasion	perseverance	psychiatry
occupant	persistence	psychology
occur	persuade	publicly
occurred	persuasive	purchase
occurrence	pertinent	pursue
occurring	pessimistic	purveyor
offered	physical	qualitative
offering	planning	quantitative
official	plausible	quantity
often	pleasant	questionnaire
omission	pleasure	quota
omitted	possession	readily
opinion	possible	readjustment
opponent	posthumous	realize
opportunity	practical	reasonable
optional	practically	receipt
ordinary	practice	receivable
organization	precedence	receive
organize	precision	receiver
original	predominant	recently
originate	preempt	receptacle
overdue	preexisting	recognize
overrun	preferable	recommend
paid	preference	reconcile
pamphlet	preferred	recur
parallel	prejudice	recurrence
partial	preliminary	recurring
participant	premium	reestablish
particular	preparation	reexamine
patience	prepare	refer
patronage	presence	reference
peculiar	previous	referred
penetrate	privilege	referring
perceive	probably	regrettable
percent	procedure	reimburse
perceptible	profession	reimbursement
performance	proficient	relief
permanent	programmed	relieve
permissible	prominent	reluctance

remember	somewhat	transfer
remembrance	specialize	transferable
remit	specialty	transferred
remittance	stabilize	transferring
remunerate	statistics	traveler
renewal	statute	truly
repetition	strategy	twelfth
representative	strictly	typical
requirement	subcommittee	ultimately
rescind	submitted	unanimous
resistance	subscriber	undoubtedly
responsibility	subsequent	unduly
responsible	subsidiary	unfortunately
restaurant	subsistence	unnecessary
reversible	substantial	until
rhythm	substantially	unusually
roofs	subtle	urgent
route	successful	usable
salable	succession	useful
salary	sufficient	usually
satellite	superintendent	vacancy
satisfactorily	supersede	validate
satisfying	supervisor	valuable
schedule	supervisory	various
secretary	supplementary	vehicle
securities	supposedly	vendor
seize	susceptible	viewpoint
semiannual	tariff	visible
sense	taxable	waive
separate	technician	warehouse
separation	technique	warranted
serviceable	tedious	weather
several	temperament	Wednesday
severely	temporarily	weigh
shipment	temporary	whether
significant	tenant	wholly
similar	tendency	withhold
simultaneous	testimonies	witnessed
sincerely	throughout	worthwhile
sincerity	tragedy	yield
sizable		

And there is no such word as:

alright	interpretative	orientate
foreward	irregardless	preventative

RESOURCES

Following is a subjective list of materials in various media that are useful to business writers.

Dictionary	*Webster's Ninth New Collegiate Dictionary.* Springfield, Mass.: Merriam-Webster, 1987.
	Webster's New World Dictionary, 3rd College Edition. New York: Webster's New World, 1988.
General Reference Books	*Concise Columbia Encyclopedia,* 2nd edition. New York: Columbia University Press, 1989. An excellent one-volume encyclopedia.
	Information Please Almanac. Boston: Houghton-Mifflin. Published each year.
	World Almanac and Book of Facts. New York: Scripps-Howard. Published each year.
	The New York Public Library Desk Reference. New York: Webster's New World, 1988.
Grammar and Usage	William A. Sabin. *Gregg Reference Manual,* 6th edition. New York: Gregg Division, McGraw-Hill, 1990.
	Webster's Dictionary of English Usage. Springfield, Mass.: Merriam-Webster, 1989.
	Dianna Booher. *Good Grief, Good Grammar: A Business Person's Guide to Grammar and Usage.* New York: Facts on File, 1988.

Karen E. Gordon. *The Transitive Vampire: A Handbook of Grammar for the Innocent, the Eager, and the Doomed*. New York: Times Books, 1984. Proof that grammar can be fun.

On Writing

William Strunk, Jr., and E. B. White. *Elements of Style,* 3rd edition. New York: Macmillan, 1979. A small book with timeless wisdom.

Rudolph Flesch. *The ABC of Style: A Guide to Plain English*. New York: Harper & Row, 1964. The seminal book by the pioneer of simple writing.

Laura Brill. *Business Writing Quick and Easy,* 2nd edition. New York: AMACOM, 1989.

Audio Tapes

Dr. Elizabeth Neeld. "Yes You Can Write." An audio cassette program on the process of writing; six tapes. From Nightingale Conant, 7300 N. Lehigh Ave., Chicago, Ill. 60648. Telephone 800-647-0300.

"The Verbal Advantage" and "The New Verbal Advantage." Two twelve-tape programs that build vocabulary and word usage skills. From Achievement Dynamics, 27751 La Paz Rd., Laguna Niguel, Cal. 92656-3919. Telephone 714-643-3011.

Software Programs

Right Writer. This grammar checker for IBM and PC clones comes packaged with a copy of Strunk and White's classic book, *Elements of Style*. From Que Software, 11711 N. College Ave., Carmel, Ind. 46032. Telephone 800-992-0244.

Word Processing
Aids

Robert W. Harris. *The DOS, Word-Perfect, and Lotus Office Companion.* Chapel Hill, N.C.: Ventana Press, 1990. A one-volume guide to the most popular software programs.

Charles O. Stewart. *Mastering WordPerfect 5.1.* Carmel, Ind.: Que Corporation, 1990. Que publishes a line of "how-to-use-your-software" guides for most of the leading business software packages.

Margaret Cole and Sylvia Oden-walk. *Desktop Presentations.* New York: AMACOM, 1990. A buyer's guide to desktop publishing software and hardware.